trumpet solos

sheet music

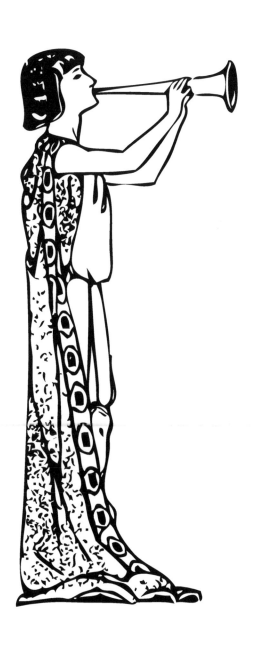

Table Of Contents

Alexander Goedicke

Russian Composer, 1877-1957

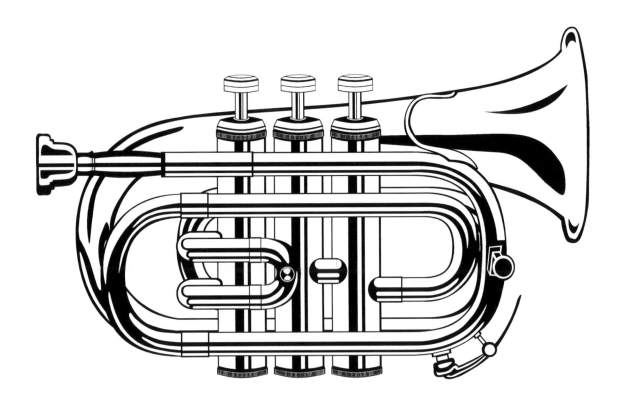

Concert Etude

Claude

Debussy

French Composer, 1862-1918

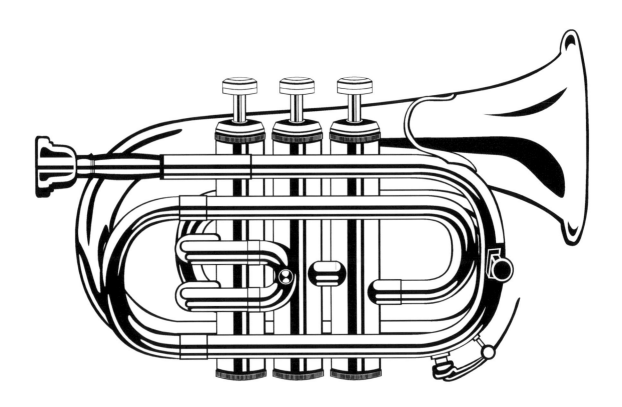

Morceau de Concours

G. ALARY
Op.57

Arabesque 1

For Solo Trumpet

Claude Debussy

Clair De Lune
For Solo Trumpet

Claude Debussy

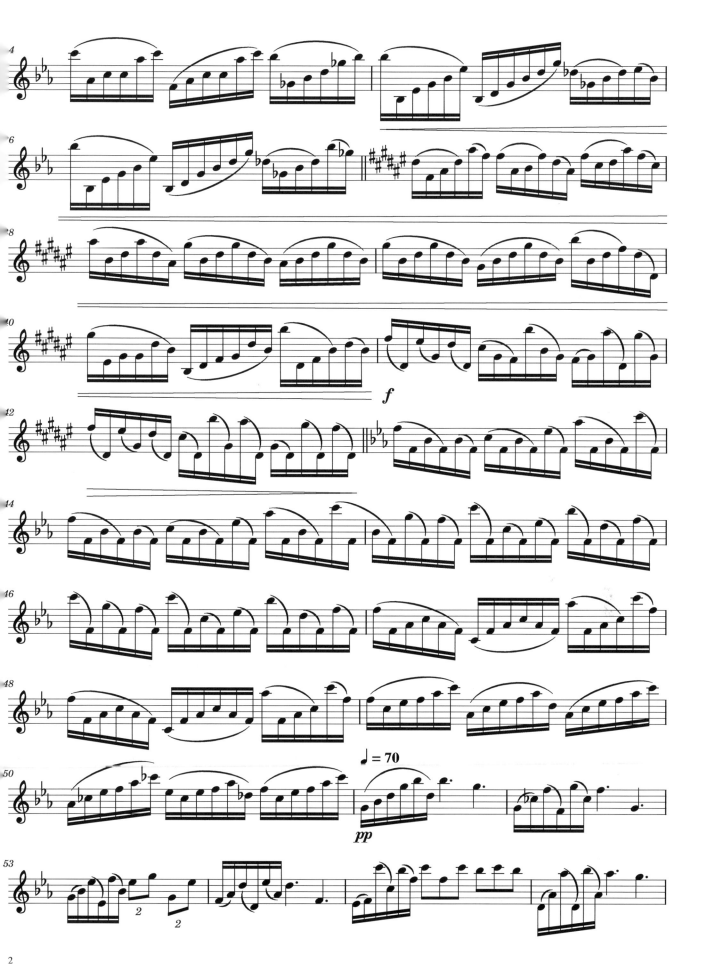

Edward Llewellyn

American Composer, 1879-1936

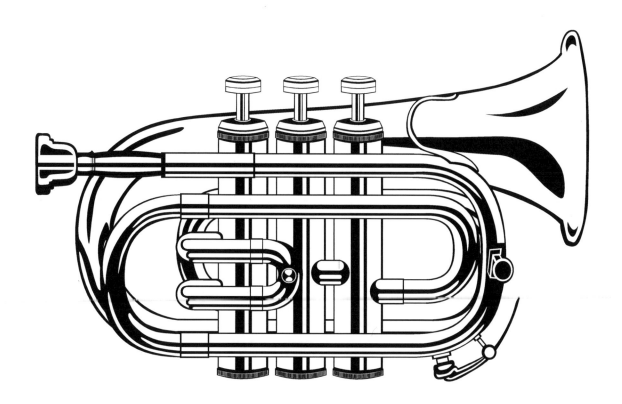

"The Premier" Polka

Cornet Solo

Edward Llewellyn

15

Frederic Weatherly

English Author & Songwriter, 1848-1929

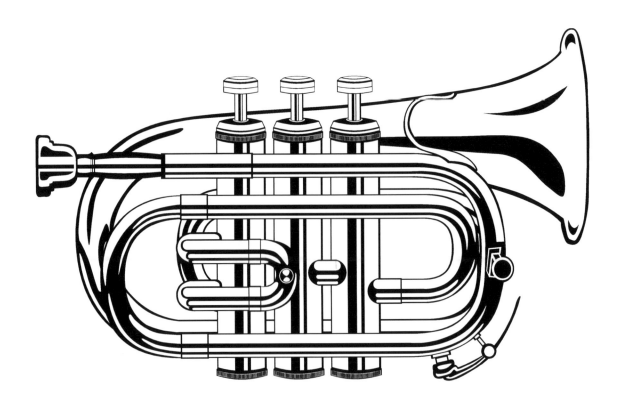

Danny Boy

Fritz Kreisler

Austrian-American Composer , 1875-1962

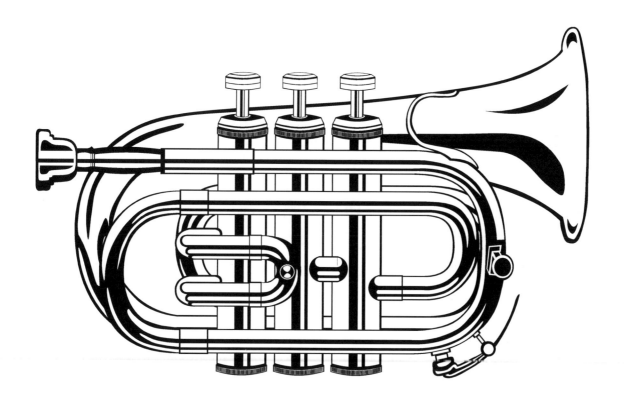

Liebesleid

Gioachino
Rossini

Italian Composer , 1792-1868

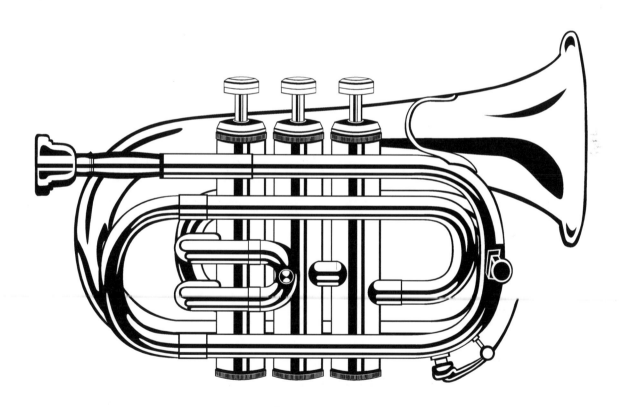

William Tell

Gioachino Rossini

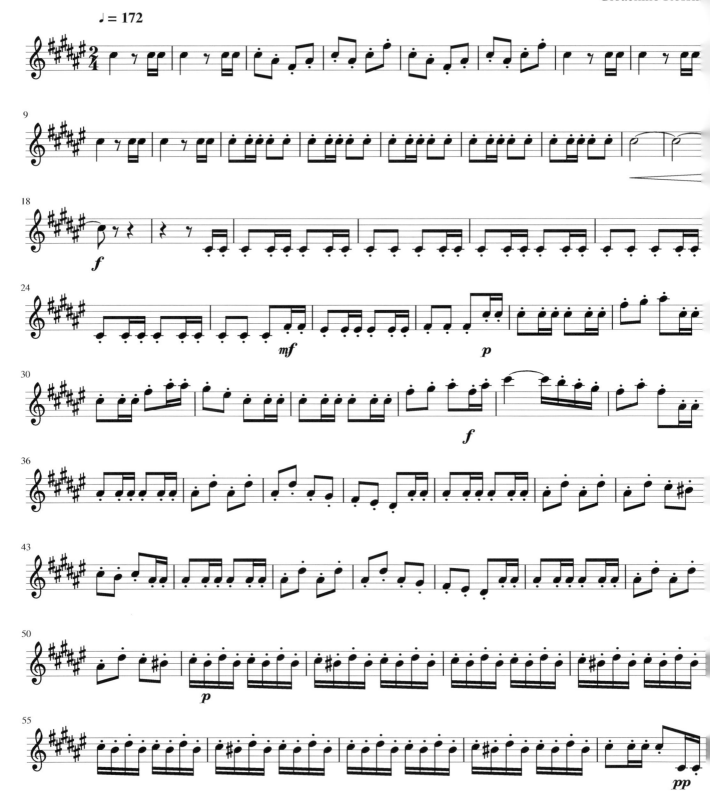

Guglielmo Tell

Ouverture - Parte Finale - (1829) Gioachino Rossini (1792 - 1868)

Johann
Pachelbel

German Composer , 1653-1706

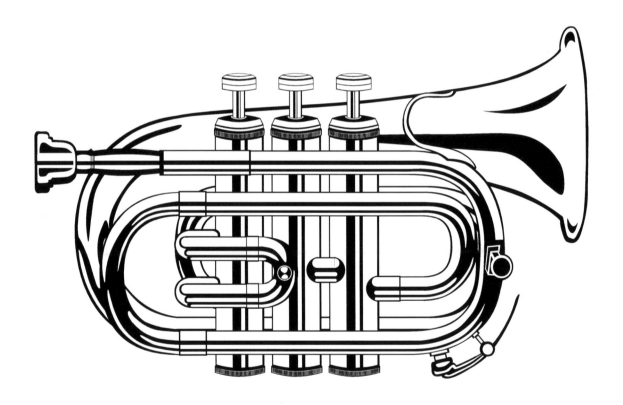

Canon in D

for Solo Trumpet

Johann PACHELBEL

Johann
Sebastian Bach

German Composer , 1685-1750

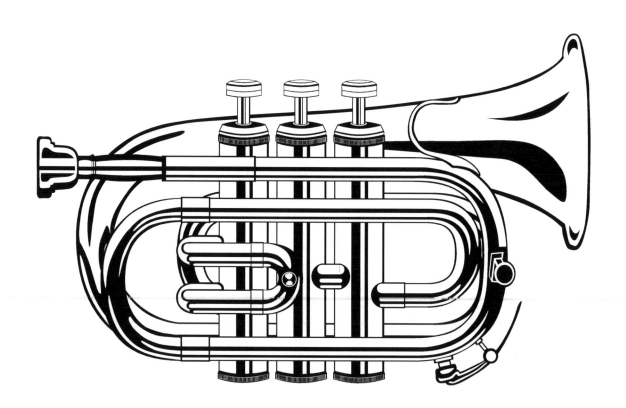

Toccata and Fugue, in D Minor
for Solo Trumpet

J. S. Bach
Michał Wolski

TOCCATA

FUGUE

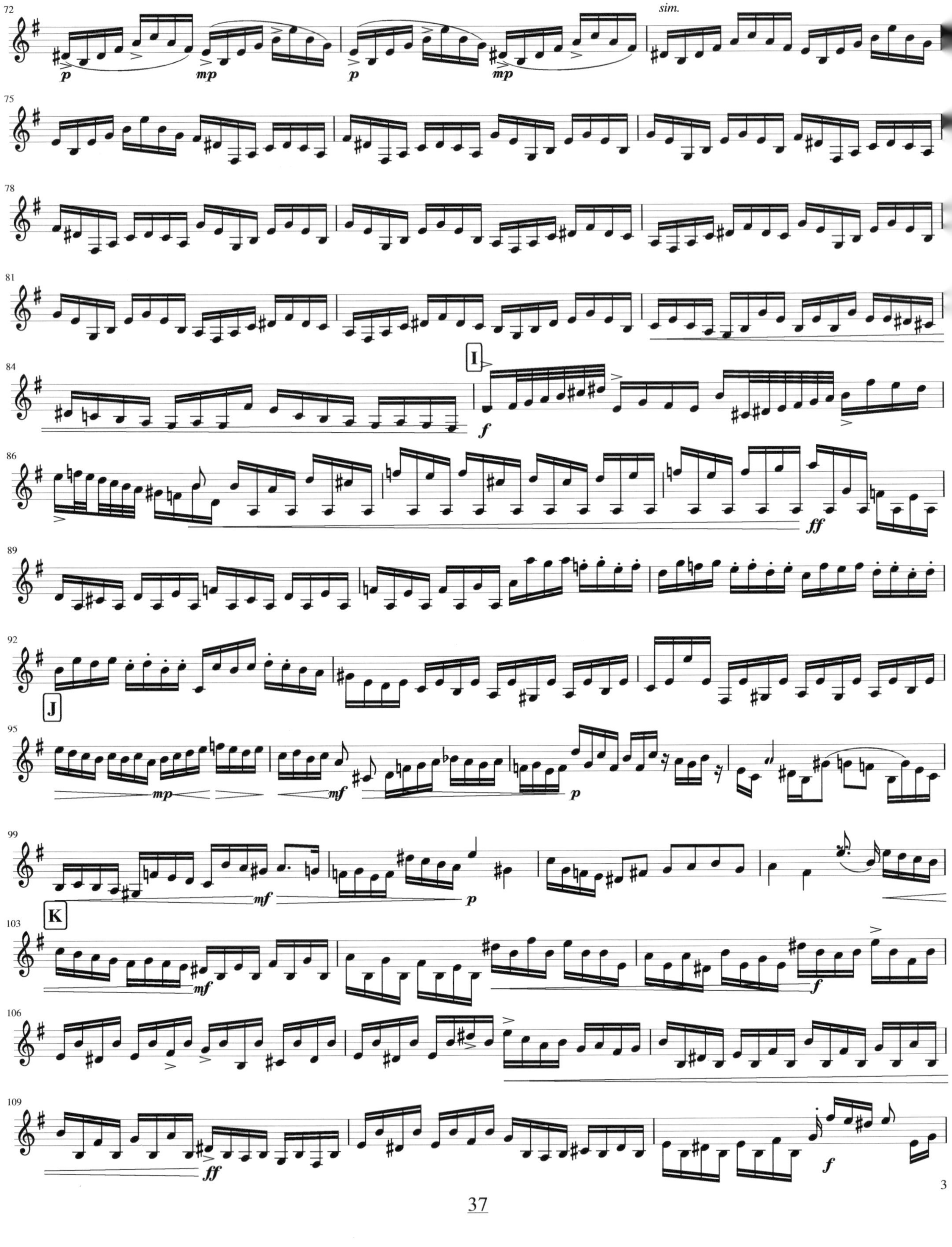
sim.
I
J
K

Little Fugue in G Minor

Johann Sebastian Bach

Minuet

J.S. Bach

Joseph Haydn

Austrian Composer , 1732-1809

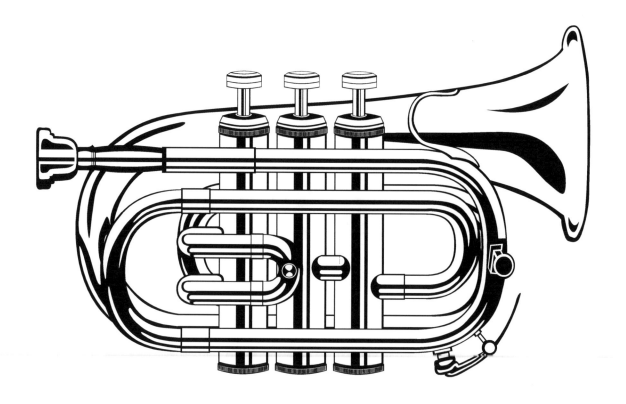

Trumpet Etude 2

Joseph Haydn

43

Concerto Cadenza

Joseph Haydn

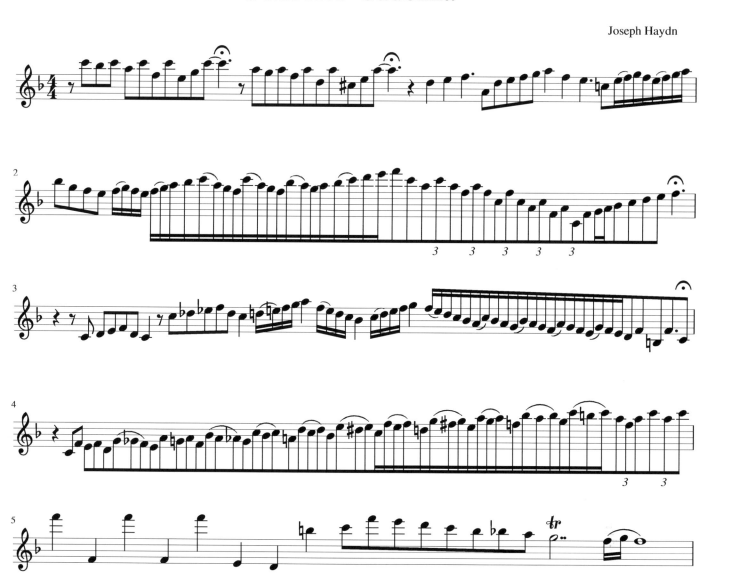

Allegro I

Joseph Haydn

Concerto III

Joseph Haydn

2

Ludwig van Beethoven

German Composer , 1770-1827

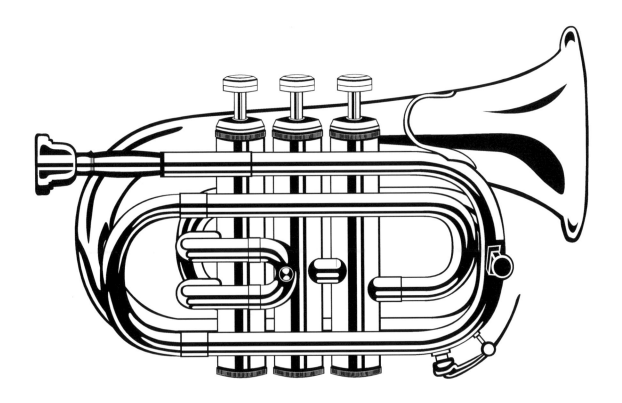

Für Elise

Niccolò

Paganini

Italian Violinist , 1782-1840

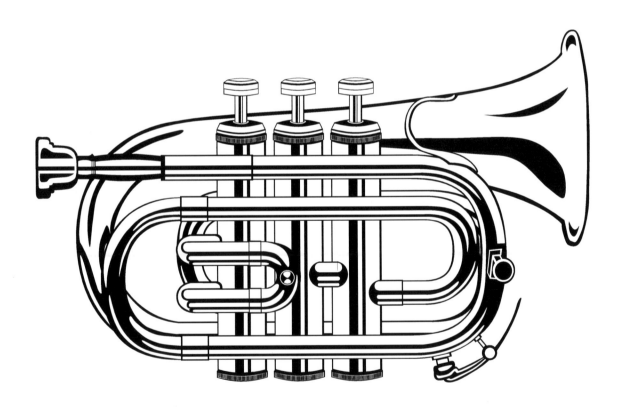

Caprice No. 24

N. Paganini

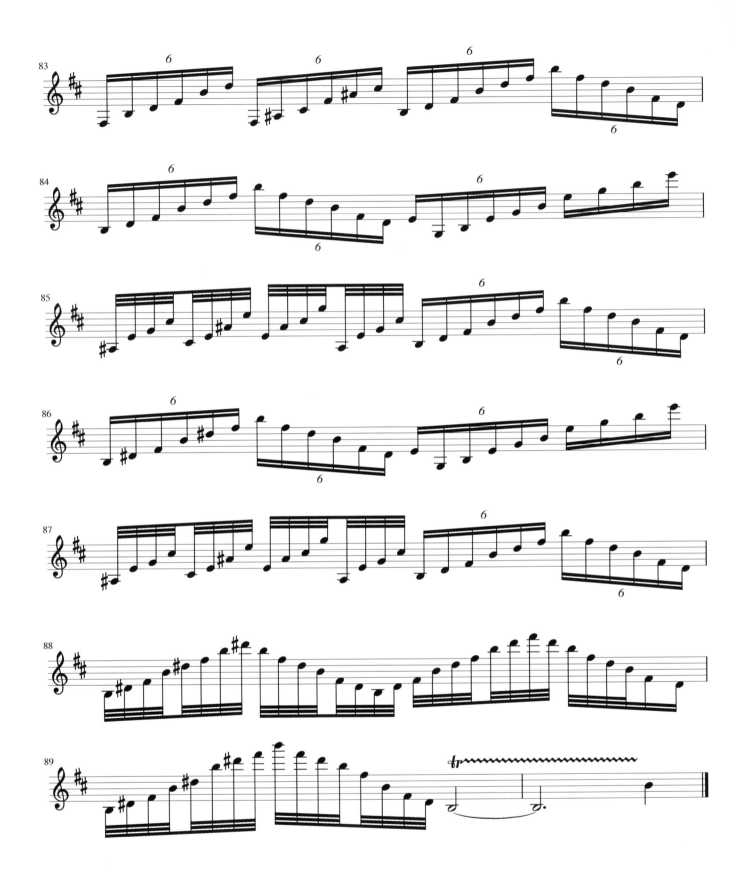

Nikolai Rimsky-Korsakov

Russian Composer , 1844-1908

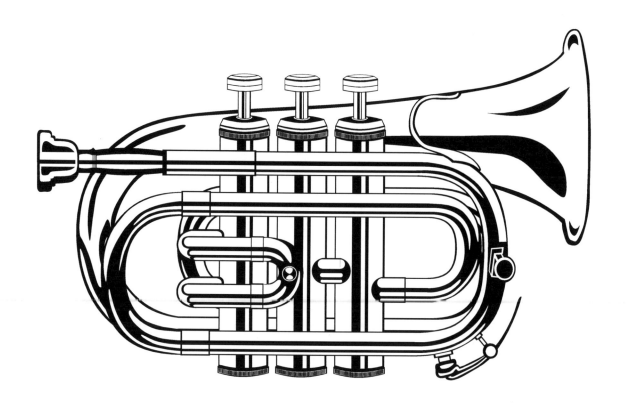

Flight of The Bumblebee

B♭ Trumpet

Nikolai Rimsky-Korsakov

Scott Joplin
American Composer , 1868-1917

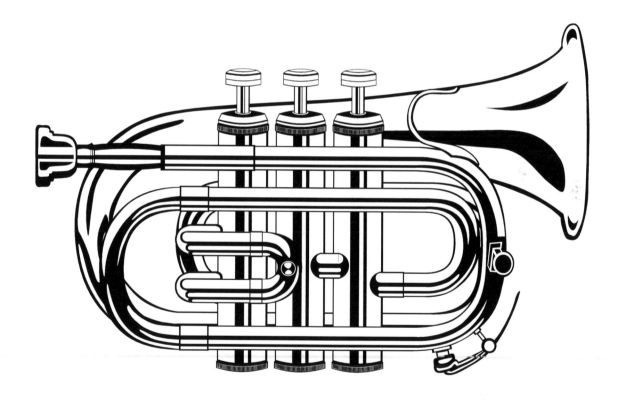

Maple Leaf Rag

The Entertainer

Wolfgang
Amadeus Mozart
Austrian Composer, 1756-1791

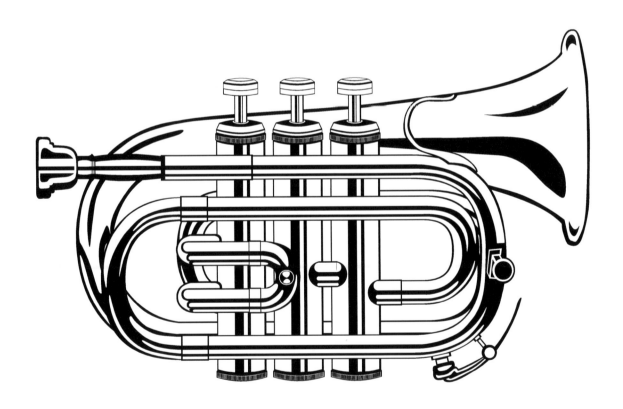

Rondo Alla Turca

Zequinha de Abreu

Brazilian Composer , 1868-1917

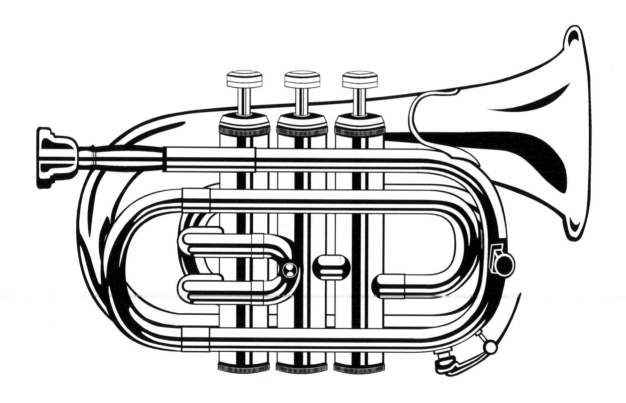

Tico Tico

Trumpet Bb

Zequinha de Abreu

Made in the USA
Middletown, DE
12 September 2023

38420799R00042